UNFINISHED BUSINESS
BUSINESS
A 1905 ESSAY

Books by Virginia Cary Hudson

O Ye Jigs & Juleps! (Macmillan Company, 1962)
Credos & Quips (Macmillan Company, 1964)
Flapdoodle, Trust & Obey (Harper & Row, 1966)
Close Your Eyes When Praying (Harper & Row, 1968)

Selected books by Beverly Mayne Kienzle

Virginia Cary Hudson, The Jigs & Juleps! Girl: Her Life and Writings
The Solutions to 38 Questions of Hildegard of Bingen (translator)
A Handbook to Hildegard of Bingen (coeditor)
A Handbook to Catherine of Siena (coeditor)
The Gospel Homilies of Hildegard of Bingen (translator)
Hildegard of Bingen and Her Gospel Homilies: Speaking New Mysteries
Expositiones evangeliorum by Hildegard of Bingen (coeditor)
Cistercians, Heresy and Crusade (1145–1229): Preaching in the Lord's Vineyard
The Sermon (editor)
Women Preachers and Prophets Through Two Millennia of Christianity (coeditor)
Medieval Sermons and Society: Cloister, City, University (coeditor)
Models of Holiness in Medieval Sermons (coeditor)
Sermons for the Summer Season: Liturgical Sermons from Rogationtide and Pentecost by Bernard of Clairvaux (translator)
De Ore Domini: Preacher and Word in the Middle Ages (coeditor)

Unfinished Business
A 1905 Essay

VIRGINIA CARY HUDSON

Author of *O Ye Jigs and Juleps!*

Edited with an introduction by

Beverly Cary Mayne Kienzle

UNFINISHED BUSINESS
A 1905 ESSAY

ISBN-13: 978-0692866726 (Beverly Cary Mayne Kienzle)
ISBN-10: 0692866728

Virginia Hudson Cleveland Mayne (1916-1989)
in the early 1960s

DEDICATION

For my mother
Virginia Cleveland Mayne,
whose loving work I continue,
whose determination and perseverance I cherish

Timeline of selected events

May 28, 1894—Virginia Cary Hudson is born in Versailles, Kentucky, the only child of Jessie G. Hudson and Richard N. Hudson V.

She spends her childhood in Cloverport and Versailles.

She attends Margaret Hall School, Versailles, and the Bristol School for Girls, Washington, DC.

January 1, 1906—R. N. Hudson is named general manager of the Louisville and Atlantic Railroad.

May 7, 1914—Virginia marries Kirtley S. Cleveland at St. John's Episcopal Church, Versailles.

January 1915—R. N. Hudson is elected president of the L. H. & St. L. Railway.

1929—L. H. & St. L. is consolidated with L. & N. R. N. Hudson becomes staff officer for operation of the L & N.

December 19, 1936—R. N. Hudson has his last meal at Pendennis Club.

January 25, 1937—R. N. Hudson dies during the great flood.

July 8, 1938—Jessie G. Hudson purchases 1453 St. James Court, Louisville.

January 22, 1942—Jessie G. Hudson dies.

1948–1954—Virginia gives talks to Women's Auxiliary at Calvary Episcopal Church and to adult Sunday classes.

Thursday, April 8, 1954—Virginia dies.

Easter Monday, April 12, 1954—Virginia's funeral is held at Olsen Funeral Home.

Easter Monday, April 16, 1962—*O Ye Jigs & Juleps!* is published.

May 27, 1962—*O Ye Jigs & Juleps!* appears on the *New York Times* Best Sellers list.

CONTENTS

ACKNOWLEDGMENTS

I am deeply grateful to Christopher Jarvinen for his generous donation to The Filson Historical Society to support The Hudson Papers Collection. His continuing friendship and encouragement animate my work. I am most appreciative that The Filson Historical Society, notably James Holmberg, Curator of Collections, established The Hudson Family Papers Collection. I am also indebted to Jennifer Cole, Manager of Collections Access, for administering the donation and to Kathryn Bratcher, Associate Curator of Collections, Filson Historical Society, for genealogical work that identified Versailles, Kentucky residents mentioned in the essay. I also thank the Kentucky Historical Society, Historical Resources, especially Sara Elliott, Director, and Beth Caffery Carter, Collections Manager, for their keen and careful attention to The Virginia Cary Hudson Collection and for permission to use photos from the collection. I am very thankful for the expert assistance of Darlene-Marie Slagle, with her careful attention and suggestions to my text as well as her empathetic and creative input to the formulation of my thoughts. I acknowledge gratefully Katherine Wrisley Shelby's contribution to organizing seemingly limitless folders and materials when she worked as my research assistant. I express my gratitude to Benjamin Adjetey for his expert editing and retouching of photos more than a century old. I appreciate Michael M. Conti's permission to use my author photo, a clip from his 2014 documentary film, "The Unruly Mystic: Saint Hildegard of Bingen." Finally, I thank Kathleen Kienzle and Edward Kienzle for their loving listening, laughter, ideas, and eagle-eyed proof-reading. The Kienzle small animals, Mia, Cecilia, Stella, and Ruby, joined the humans in moments of merriment, amusement, and affection.

Introduction, Part One
O Ye Jigs & Juleps!

Asmall book of ten delightful essays rocked the publishing world in 1962 and reached the *New York Times Book Review*'s Best Seller List in less than two months. The bestselling *O Ye Jigs & Juleps!* contained insightful and humorous writings by a 10-year-old child, Virginia Cary Hudson, my beloved grandmother. For readers who need a refresher on the amazing story of *O Ye Jigs & Juleps!*, I retell it briefly below in the first half of the Introduction.

You may be astonished to learn that there is an essay missing from *O Ye Jigs & Juleps!*, an eleventh essay that I discovered not long ago. My grandmother wrote it during the same period and under the same circumstances as the published essays. You have questions, I'm sure. How could that happen? How could an essay by Virginia Cary Hudson remain unknown? When and where did I find it?

My mother, Virginia Cleveland Mayne, published the best-selling book and three other slim volumes of my grandmother's writings after my grandmother's death. I inherited all the papers related to the publications and family business after my mother died in 1989 in Florida, where she and my father had lived since 1971. My father safeguarded seemingly countless folders, bags, and boxes until they all arrived at my home in Massachusetts. I was then beginning to write academic papers and establish myself as a professor. That process continued relentlessly for over thirty years. Collaboration with colleagues built an expanding web of unexplored topics for research and fostered sustaining friendships that led me to further projects. I enjoyed the work, I deeply appreciated the collegiality, and I still cherish the friends I made. So many projects created too many deadlines, and the pace of writing rarely slowed until I hit the brakes and decided to retire from new academic projects as well as from my professorship.

After retirement, I confronted the piles of papers and other materials that my mother accumulated: bulging folders snugly wrapped with double knotted strings and held by double layers of tightly stretched rubber bands. Inside those were enclosed more folders containing loose papers, newspaper reviews, letter drafts, flyers, and plastic bags of varying sizes. Tucked inside every large bundle lay an envelope filled with the four-leaf clovers that my mother managed to find everywhere she went. I was foraging for sources that I could use in writing the biography of my grandmother, *Virginia Cary Hudson, The Jigs & Juleps! Girl: Her Life and Writings* (2016).

After finishing the biography, I located an ordinary looking folder that contained writings in my grandmother's hand. I had recognized most of the titles as her adult essays that had already been published. I looked again, just to be sure that I had not missed something. I discovered a short essay, written in my grandmother's hand and dated 1905, that is during my grandmother's 10th to 11th year! Wow! I panicked! How did I miss something so important? Wait! Was she 10 or 11 years old? Ten, because she wrote the essay during Lent and her birthday is May 28, 1894. What should I do with an essay that demonstrates her age so clearly? I have been mulling that over for almost two years now. This little book, devoted to the eleventh essay, "The Business World," is the answer. I publish the text here after providing a context for it in the second part of the Introduction.

I include never-before-seen photos from the house in Versailles, Kentucky, where my grandmother lived at the age when she wrote the essays in *O Ye Jigs & Juleps!* I remembered seeing very old photos in the 1960s, but I could not find them anywhere in my piles of folders. It was not until 2016 that I visited the archives at the Kentucky Historical Society in Frankfort, where my mother had sent other donations in the mid-1970s. When I saw the carefully preserved photos there, I realized that several of them date from my grandmother's childhood and precisely from the period when she lived in Versailles and wrote the now famous essays.

Attic treasure saved from a fire

My mother and my grandmother discovered the essays in May 1952 while exploring the attic in my grandmother's home at 1453 St. James Court in Louisville. They copied them by hand and typewriter during my family's annual visit for the Kentucky Derby. Several months later--October 16, 1952, a devastating fire in the attic destroyed the essays and other papers. Fortunately, my mother had taken the copies home to Maryland after the Derby visit. Less than a year later, on April 8, 1954, my grandmother suddenly passed away from a heart attack, while talking with a friend on the phone.

Rejection and persistence

My mother promised herself that she would publish the essays and other adult writings by her mother. She worked tirelessly for several years to achieve her goal, but she received only rejection letters—17 of them. The dining room of our home in Maryland served as her office; a 1908 typewriter functioned as her press. To reach the nearest Post Office and a store that sold typing paper, my mother walked about a mile and a half, partly along the route I took to school. I often accompanied her. Sometimes she met me at my school and we would walk home together. Believing firmly that my mother would succeed, I moved her spirit from worried anticipation of failure to hopeful expectation of success. My mother loosened the reins of playful daydreams that rested in her heart. Carried by a burst of cheerful reveries, we picked up the pace as we neared the post office and imagined what would happen if the papers in the brown mailing envelope really became a book. Then we waited for news.

To produce the manuscript copies that we mailed, my mother patiently guided layers of onion-skin paper and carbons into her 1908 typewriter, rolling them slowly and carefully. Why the onion skins? For manuscript submission, my mother needed to send an original plus a "photostat" copy. The onion skins provided her own copies. Photostat copies were costly and not readily accessible in the 1950s, before the advent of the plain paper Xerox machine in 1960. The expense to have the photostats made included the bus fare for a 30-

minute trip into Washington, DC, where she could find a printing shop. The Greyhound bus traveled along Route 450 from the Maryland suburbs into the District and made a stop at 9:03 a.m. about half a mile from our house.

When manuscripts were rejected and returned, we checked them for markings or frayed edges. A damaged manuscript could not be submitted again. My mother would need to make another trip on the "nine o'three." What did we do with piles of extra manuscripts? There weren't enough table tops or shelves to hold them. My mother stored papers under chairs when there was no room anywhere else. She hung a "Bless this Mess" sign in the living room and explained to guests, with playfully raised eyebrows and a disarming smile, that the piles were accent pieces to make the house feel "lived in." Being at odds with the late 1950s--early 1960s model of the housewife did not concern her. She regularly quoted Phyllis Diller, her favorite comedian, on the usefulness of dust bunnies and heaps.

My mother's only assistant, I proofread and helped to separate the layers of carbons and onion skins. I delighted in verifying spelling and in checking finished pages. Spelling was my sport and spelling bees my playing fields. Sometimes I typed the manuscript pages, but with great caution. A mistake meant redoing the entire page and the onion skin copies. I grew in reverence for words, pages, and manuscripts. For as long as I remember, I wanted to grow up to be a teacher. Little did I foresee that, before me in my dining room, I was preparing for a life of writing and publishing. When I look back through the eyes of a nearly seventy-year-old, I see that I became accustomed to books at a young age, not just reading them but making them, getting them from written pages to a printed and bound object to hold in the hand!

The process of typing the essays, duplicating them, mailing the envelopes, and waiting for a reply continued until 1961. I was away at school from 1959 to 1963. Letters and occasional phone calls substituted poorly for daily conversations and mail deliveries. I was anxious for news and worried about my mother. A friend of my mother helped her by typing more copies of the manuscript and distributing them to friends.

One copy of the manuscript reached Catherine, the wife of Angus Dun, Episcopal Bishop of Washington, DC. "Kitty" loved the essays and identified with Virginia, who reminded Kitty in many ways of herself at the same age. Mrs. Dun took the manuscript straightaway to Doris Thompson and Martha Johnson, literary agents who owned the Francis Scott Key Bookshop in Georgetown. Diplomats and members of Congress, even Secretary of State Dean Acheson, frequented the quaint townhouse, as did Washington journalists such as Walter Lippman.

Publication

With a Macmillan Company contract in hand by May 1961, my mother waited for publication the next year. In February 1962, prepublication reviews began to appear. Advance orders for the fifty-page book then flooded the Macmillan Company. The prestigious publisher moved the publication date from late May to April 16, 1962, Monday of Holy Week. That day marked eight years, according to liturgical time, after my grandmother's burial on Monday of Holy Week in 1954. By April 30, 1962, when the *Newsweek* review appeared, the book was already in its third printing. The esteemed critic Lewis Nichols praised the book in the *New York Times Book Review* on May 13, 1962, doubtless boosting the demand for copies. Two weeks later, on May 27, the day before Virginia Cary Hudson would have celebrated her 68th birthday, the collection of essays reached the *New York Times Book Review*'s Best Seller List. "The sleeper bestseller of the season," as *Newsweek* called *O Ye Jigs & Juleps!*, kept selling and held a place on the esteemed Best Seller List for 66 weeks. "Delightful is the word for it, whoever you are," wrote Lewis Nichols. He observed that, "Some of Virginia's thoughts sound as though Machiavelli had rewritten Emily Post—to the greater good and glory of all concerned."

Readers of *O Ye Jigs & Juleps!* delighted at Virginia's many escapades – baptizing in a rain barrel, pouring paint over a boy's head, rambunctious pony rides, jumping fences, drinking too much wine at a neighbor's house, and fighting with a girl who insulted St. Paul. Virginia recounted her captivating adventures and described her world with a remarkable sense of humor and an acute perception of human behavior. Her view encompassed the residents of her small Southern town, from Morgan Street, home of the rough and ready Campbellites, to Rose Hill, where Mrs. Haggin resided, the second wife of James Ben Ali Haggin, at one time the third richest man in the United States. Between those two addresses, Virginia captured her observations of other residents, including the loudly-singing Baptists, the blue-stocking Presbyterians, the Episcopalians who were so stuck-up that they could "strut sitting down," the black boys who taught her to dance, the librarian with her children and patrons, a drunken neighbor, the lovelorn, and the pesky Neville Graddy who put red pepper under her pony's tail.

Virginia's spirited descriptions of life in her town attracted over one million readers, in hardback and paperback editions. My mother published three more collections of my grandmother's adult writings in 1964, 1966, and 1968: *Credos & Quips, Flapdoodle, Trust & Obey*, and *Close Your Eyes When Praying.* She spoke around the country at book events with famous authors such as Barbara Tuchman and Theodore C. Sorensen, and she appeared on the *Today* show in February 1965 for an interview with Barbara Walters.

None of the three books above attained the popularity of *O Ye Jigs & Juleps*! Yet its acclaim stirred up doubts among a few contentious reviewers. My mother was crushed to learn that *Time* magazine intended to prove the essays were not written by Virginia Cary Hudson. A *Time* representative sat insolently in the doorway of the Francis Scott Key Bookshop, insisting that he would return and remain every day until Martha and Doris, the shop's owners and my mother's agents, admitted that the essays were fake. But the *Time* representative eventually had to depart, faced with a complete lack of evidence for his claims. He had even alleged that the October 1952 fire did not happen, and he contemptuously barked at my mother that it was a "convenient fire." She procured a letter from the insurance company to prove that the fire took place. Finally, rumors circulated that my grandmother never existed, an even more heart-breaking charge against the integrity of my mother, a woman who loved her mother deeply and worked tirelessly to preserve her memory. Sadly, my mother never recovered from that attack. Her voice broke every time she recounted the story.

Introduction, Part Two
"The Business World"

T he question returns then: Why did my mother omit one essay? What does the material evidence show? There are two copies of the essay, one transcribed in my grandmother's adult hand, the other typed, presumably by my mother, when they worked together in May 1952 to copy the original essays after finding them in the attic. My grandmother's copy is written, as were many of her adult works, with pencil on pages torn from a spiral composition book. The date of 1905 appears in the upper left corner, also in my grandmother's adult writing. The typed copy, on paper turning brown and dry, has seven pages plus one paragraph on the eighth page. Therefore, the essay corresponds to other drafts of my grandmother's writings in its material, that is composition notebook and pencil. Additionally and very significantly, it bears the date, written in the same hand—my grandmother's—of 1905.

What else stands out about the unpublished 11th essay? Like the chapters in *O Ye Jigs & Juleps!*, "The Business World" shows the structure of a school composition. In this case, an opening paragraph deals with nine categories of business and focuses on the ninth, unfinished business. The composition-like format of the writing aligns it clearly with the ten essays in *O Ye Jigs & Juleps!* Note that the numbering in the copies made from the original does not add up to the number of business types. My grandmother most likely misnumbered the types at some point, writing the number five twice for two separate and distinct categories and omitting the number seven altogether.

What does Virginia Cary Hudson understand about "The Business World" at the age of ten? Virginia lists nine categories of business. The first two types reflect the activities she observed around her as the daughter of a railroad engineer: digging and "setting off dynamite." Railways were expanding in the early twentieth century, and bridges were being built across rivers wide and narrow. Virginia mentions bridges and tells in *O Ye Jigs & Juleps!* that neighbors in

Versailles complained about the dynamite blasts that cleared the way for construction.

Virginia's father (my great-grandfather), Richard N. Hudson V, worked as a civil engineer. Jessie Hudson's handwritten obituary for her husband recounts that Richard worked under Col. Patton of the renowned Civil Engineers. William MacFarland Patton (1845–1905), studied at what is now Virginia Tech, established himself as a leading engineer for bridge construction and later became a professor at his *alma mater*. My great-grandfather served as road master and chief resident engineer for the Louisville, Henderson, and St. Louis Railway Company (then known as the Louisville, St. Louis and Texas Railway Company), and he was resident engineer in Cloverport, Kentucky. He was named general manager of the Louisville and Atlantic Railroad on January 1, 1906. He traveled locally by railway on business and Virginia met him at the train station in Versailles. He also made a trip to New York to discuss a trolley deal, writing to Jessie on December 19, 1906, from the Waldorf-Astoria.

In January 1915, R. N. Hudson was elected president of the L. H. & St. L. Railway. The family moved from Cloverport, residence of Jessie's parents and relatives and site of the the L. H. & St. L. work yards, to Versailles, and finally to Louisville after Hudson accepted the position as president.

The photo on the opposite page shows my great-grandfather's home office at the family house in Versailles. Richard N. Hudson is sitting at the desk on the right in front of the window. The other two men are not identified. The photo dates from around 1905, as do others included in this book.

Returning to Virginia's nine categories of business, we see that she writes, "No. 1" is "working business. That's when you dig all day." Number 2 is railroad business, and that is "setting off dynamite." Business categories 3 and 4 in the essay relate to money, that is banking and giving to the church. The next three types pertain to talking or not talking: "Other people's business" (5), "Everybody's business" (labeled 5 but should be 6), and "Nobody's business" (labeled 6 but should be 7). "Your own business," as in scrubbing yourself, is number 8. The last type of business (9) Virginia describes in this way: "your unfinished business. That's when you better start thinking. And this is about my unfinished business I am writing."

At the end of the composition, a note on the page indicates that Virginia's local bishop remarked approvingly, "Most worthy abstinence." This comment indicates that the bishop evaluated the essay. Why did a bishop comment on Virginia's essay? The main actions in this composition take place on Ash Wednesday and Easter

Day, the beginning and the end of the Lenten season. Old time Episcopalians took the forty days of Lent very seriously. They followed the monastic tradition for Lenten study and the ancient practice of Lenten preparation for reception into the church. Such preparation developed into a program of study for confirmation in the years prior to receiving the sacrament itself. That involved extra composition writing for older children and even a contest for the best essay. Virginia attended an Episcopal school, so religious topics for assignments would be a matter of course. There was an additional emphasis on theological lessons, however simple, during Lent. In addition, people were instructed to abstain from, that is give up, something they liked or wanted to do. They practiced different forms of abstinence. In my house, we abstained from meat on both Wednesdays and Fridays. A more personal regime might entail giving up bubble gum or soda or chocolate, or in Virginia's case, retaliation against Neville Graddy's pranks. That restraint was Virginia's Lenten abstinence.

Virginia waits for Easter Day to take her final action in the essay. She gets revenge on Neville Graddy by hitting him with a sock full of marbles! What did Neville Graddy do? On Ash Wednesday, he poured hot red pepper under the tail of Virginia's pony and sent the poor creature running wildly. Virginia jumped on the pony, riding him bareback, to the cistern. The pony eventually calmed down when she poured water on the area under his tail, rinsing off the pepper.

The Lenten framework for the essay along with the invaluable date of 1905 reveal that Virginia Cary Hudson was not far from her eleventh birthday, May 28, 1905. She was awaiting confirmation in the Episcopal Church the following year. This essay and others clearly show that she had not yet received it. In "China and Religion" she writes, "Next year Bishop Burton is going to make me an Episcopalian" (*O Ye Jigs & Juleps!* 49). Her confirmation must have taken place in 1906, when she turned twelve. If the service of confirmation took place before May 28, 1906, her twelfth birthday, the Bishop customarily would have allowed her to be confirmed a tiny bit early. Therefore, "The Business World" soundly demonstrates that Virginia was ten years old although approaching her 11th birthday, preparing for confirmation the next year and learning by heart the teachings of the Episcopal Church (*Articles of Instruction*).

What then caused my mother to omit "The Business World" from *O Ye Jigs & Juleps!*? Why did she omit an essay that clearly indicates my grandmother's age? First, I would say, she had no inkling that someone, anyone, would question the authenticity of my grandmother's writing, much less her identity. My mother did not publish the essays in *O Ye Jigs & Juleps!* to prove her mother's existence. Who would ever have imagined that anyone would allege after publication of the essays that a vibrant, active, creative woman such as my grandmother was an invention?

While authenticity was not on my mother's "radar," her mother's character and reputation were front and center. Virginia Cary Hudson and Kirtley S. Cleveland divorced and remarried sometime in the 1920s while living in Versailles. That news must have shaken up the small town. Any worries about reverberations from the divorce revolved around real events, including a custody battle, a kidnapping, and rumors of interested suitors eager to replace my grandfather. If such divorce stories surfaced, they actually might have confirmed Virginia's existence.

Would the young Virginia's mischievous behavior make my mother hesitate to publish "The Business World"? Virginia's antics in *O Ye Jigs & Juleps!* often resulted in punishment. In "Education," when Virginia gets sick from the abundant wine served at a neighbor's house, her mother "said plenty," and then compelled her to read "every word" of the Women's Christian Temperance book (*O Ye Jigs & Juleps!* 21). When Virginia puts a sign on the door, telling visitors to stay at home until the good dishes were unpacked, her mother "had one of her fits" (*O Ye Jigs & Juleps!* 35). After Virginia slapped a Campbellite girl for saying, "Fooie on St. Paul," her mother sat her down to read St. Paul for an hour (*O Ye Jigs & Juleps!* 42). Virginia offers a principle on fighting: "I never fight unless some brat slaps me first. Then I fold up my good hair ribbon and finish what they start" (*O Ye Jigs & Juleps!* 46). Virginia also tells of being ordered to stay in her room for four hours, because she came barefooted into the parlor to speak to the Judge, and then for four more hours, because she hit the last note of her piano piece "with her toe" (*O Ye Jigs & Juleps!* 50).

The photo below shows Virginia playing her piano with her teacher at the left and her father on the right, holding the violin he loved to play. Virginia seems to be around ten, the same age she was in the well-known picture on the cover of this book. Her hair is parted tightly here, with curls tied up in bows. The curls are loose in the cover photo, as they must have been when the bothersome Neville Graddy tied them to the choir stall, just as the choir prepared to rise for "Stand up, Stand up for Jesus."

The photo above captures Virginia in her room at the Versailles house, looking as if she had been punished. Her dress resembles the one she is wearing in the previous picture, as does her hair style. Photos of Virginia included here were found by a cousin in Alabama after the publication of *O Ye Jigs & Juleps!*

During the course of her exploits in "The Business World," Virginia receives another punishment after talking back to a bothersome neighbor. Her mother obliged her to sit and read her Bible for two hours. She loves reading about David, she says, and would like to take him to Morgan Street to fight the Campbellites. Again, Virginia is punished when she repeats to her mother what Mr. Moseley says to her, namely, "I am drunk as hell." Her mother then washed Virginia's mouth out with the soap used for washing the dog.

"The Business World" ends with Virginia receiving a hard beating from her mother Jessie, much more severe than the hours of reading that Jessie often assigned for punishment. I think that my mother might have felt uncomfortable about one of the actions in the story: either Virginia's revenge on Neville, her "unfinished business," when she whaps him with a mitten full of pebbles; or more likely, the beating her mother gave her, so hard "that her pompadour bounced loose and her rat fell out," that is the hairpiece around which the pompadour hair style was arranged. Virginia had expected a penalty of reading the Bible for hours and not a beating. She concludes unconvincingly that she does not care about the beating. "I sure finished my unfinished business," she says. "Lent is over. The Lord is risen... Glory! Hallelujah!"

"The Business World" not only shows a harsh side of Virginia's mother, but it also enhances our glimpse of life and work in Versailles. Several characters from *O Ye Jigs & Juleps!* appear, such as Virginia's friend Mrs. Hunter, who enjoys gardening and fishing with her young neighbor, to Mrs. Hunter's daughter, Ms. Pearl Haggin, who finds that Versailles "cramps her style." Virginia tells us more about her Shetland pony Scissors, a gift to Virginia from Mr. Hangar. Mr. Hangar, she says, builds bridges over the railways on Mr. Milton Smith's railroad. Mr. Smith was then President of the L. & N. Railroad. He was succeeded by Mr. Mapother, not mentioned in *O Ye Jigs & Juleps!*, who gave Virginia's father a "fine dog." Other neighborhood residents make an appearance: Mr. Moseley, and Mr. Browning, a busybody and not a favorite of Virginia's. Moreover, Virginia's father expresses his wariness of Wilhelm Hohenzollern (Wilhelm II, 1859-1941, r. 1888-1918) and the Kaiser's perceived hatred for the English—a reference to the period before World War I.

Moreover, "The Business World," like the ten essays in *O Ye Jigs & Juleps!*, reveals character traits that Virginia displayed as a child and still as an adult. Virginia knew no timidity when challenging situations arose. She was tall, 5'9" in adulthood. William, the houseboy with whom she grew up, taught her how to defend herself. That she did indeed, from childhood into adulthood. Virginia the ten-year old swung a punching bag made of a mitten and pebbles to stun a pesky boy, Neville Graddy. Virginia the fifty-year old wielded a heavy pocketbook to hit a thief in the alley behind the Salvation Army Chapel in Louisville. "Preaching on Monday and fighting in the alley on Tuesday," she concluded in a letter to my mother.

Virginia's incorporation of daily life into church teaching emerges in "The Business World." After the beating that her mother applied, Virginia showed the hope and humor that remained with her in dark situations all her life. Moreover, what makes "The Business World," remarkable and delightful is how Virginia employs the thematic framework of Lent, generally a dreary theological topic, in an essay on business and how she illustrates the serious topic of abstaining during Lent with her own hilarious and inimitable adventures.

Lenten abstinence goes hand in hand with the wait to respond to Neville Graddy. Virginia knows he does not have a mother and feels sorry for him, but he is quite a smart aleck. He tied her curls to the choir bench just before the choir began singing, "Stand up, stand up for Jesus." She did not retaliate. Then he threw red pepper under her pony's tail, but she still held back because of what the bishop taught her about abstaining during Lent. Abstaining, she says, "means getting even with people, as well as eating candy." Neville seems to have heard the same message as Virginia. All through Lent he taunted her, saying "Fraidy cat" in her face. Easter joy, explains Virginia, means that "the Lord is alive again and abstaining is over." The end of abstention results in getting even with Neville Graddy.

This Lenten tale belongs beside other manifestations in *O Ye Jigs & Juleps!* of Virginia's blending of daily life and theology. As a child, she intersperses her tales from Versailles with religious lessons, what she was learning more intensely for Confirmation. She values the Bishop's words and instruction, and she echoes lines from the *Book of Common Prayer* throughout the essays. The theological lessons endure all her life. Those teachings, the stories she uses to illustrate them, and her often humorous conclusions grow in maturity and complexity as she herself does. Sheryl A. Kujawa-Holbrook observes that Virginia writes about faith within the context of daily life, as do other women who have developed the genre of spiritual narrative. Virginia's preaching in two non-denominational chapels in Louisville may seem surprising, simply because she was female. As Zachary Guiliano explains, "Virginia was ahead of her time ... in many ... ways— not least being a woman who taught and preached regularly."

Yet Virginia's down-to-earth way of thinking and speaking explains why she was a clear choice. As the Goodwill Chapel representative said to her, "The la-di-da words of some of the robed preachers do not go over down here. These are simple and plain people who want a simple truth." Virginia delivered that truth with an abundance of down-to-earth examples that touched the hearts of her varied audiences.

The Business World

Virginia Cary Hudson

The only kind of businesses that I can think of are No. 1 working business. That's when you dig all day. No. 2. Railroad business. That's when you set off dynamite. No 3. Banking business. That's when you put your money then take it out. No. 4. The Lord's business. That's when you give money you want to keep yourself. No. 5. Other people's business. That's when you talk too much. No. 5. Everybody's business. That's when everybody talks at once, and nobody can hear a thing, like the Ladies' Aid Society that meets at our house because we have lots of chairs and cups. No. 6. Nobody's business. That's when you don't talk. 8. Your own business. That's like when you scrub yourself, and if your stomach is already clean you just skip it. No. 9. your unfinished business. That's when you better start thinking. And this is about my unfinished business I am writing.

Betty Hangar's daddy gave me a Shetland pony. That's because my father let him put his bridges over the rivers on Mr. Milton Smith's railroad. That pony is too slow for me. He does to me what Versailles does to Miss Pearl Haggin. He cramps my style. Mrs. Hunter is Miss Pearl's mother, and she told me, while we were fishing, that "Versailles sure cramps Pearl's style." Mrs. Hunter is my friend. She lets me dig her worms. I wanted a broncho, and when I save $50.00, if I ever do, Mr. John Morris is going to sell me his spotted one. He said to me, Mr. John I mean, not the broncho, he said, "I am warning you, he is wild." And I said back to him, "I am too." Only when I said that too, I should have said also.

Neville Graddy asked me why I named my pony "Scissors" and I said because I was hoping every day he would cut up. Neville is twelve years old, and he thinks he is smart. Neville doesn't have any mother, and I try my best not to sass him, but I knew that first day he tied my curls to the knob on the choir bench just before "Stand up, Stand up for Jesus," that sooner or later I was going to have to fix him. Neville asked me on Ash Wednesday why I didn't like my pony and I told him because he was too slow. And he said, "Maybe I can speed him up for you." And he sneaked in Mrs. Powhatan Woolridge's kitchen and ran out with a can of red pepper and threw it under my pony's tail, and when he started bucking and running I sure was glad I didn't have to bother with the saddle. I sure was glad my legs were long enough to wrap around his stomach. When my grandmother saw me for the first time she said, "Her legs are too long."

When I got my pony back home, I backed him up to the cistern and pumped water on him where the red pepper was. Then Mr. Browning came along. He is always coming along. He lives across the street where he can see everything that goes on. He said to me, he said "What in the world are you doing," and I was mad and I said to him, I said, "Mr. Browning I wanted to tell you for years to mind your own business, now I am telling you." And Mr. Browning rang our door bell and told my mother I was impudent and should be punished. Then my mother called me in our parlor and I was so mad I couldn't get any madder, and I told Mr. Browning if Neville did to him what he did to my pony, he would be glad for me to pump water on him, only I wouldn't do it. He could just run and buck for all I cared.

And our maid had to bring my mother her smelling salts, and I had to sit in my chair and read my Bible for two hours. I can always turn back to David and his giants. I just love David. I sure would like to see David meet Mr. Browning leading the Philistines. Only Mr. Browning would be leading the Campbellites. They are plenty tough. Those kids on Morgan Street always want to fight. When I go up in that part of town, I do like David. I take my slingshot. Maybe I can find the jawbone of an ass.

My mother says that Mr. Moseley is an ass. Maybe when he dies his wife will give me his jaw bone. One day I saw him coming home and every time he would get two steps in front he would still be behind. And I said "Lean on me, Sir, and I will help you." And I said "What is wrong with you Mr. Moseley, Sir?" And he said "Little girl I am as drunk as hell." And I ran home and said to my mother "Guess what, Mr. Moseley is as drunk as hell." And she washed my mouth out with the soap my father uses on his fine dog Mr. Mapother gave him.

My father said to me some dogs have four legs and some have two. My father makes up riddles like Samson. And he said, my father I mean not Samson, "Speaking of dogs the British had better watch that Wilhelm Hohenzollern." And I said "Why?" And my father said "Because he hates the English." And I said "Why?" and my father said "Because he was born at Victoria's castle and he blamed the English doctor for his arm being shriveled up." I bet I know how that happened. I bet the angels brought him down to his mother, the doctor jumped from behind the door and twisted his arm. Harvey Steadman told me his father, Dr. Steadman, beats you on your bottom when you are born until you yell. I guess he figures you are going to need it and he will just give it to you there.

I have already told you once that it was Ash Wednesday when Neville put red pepper under my pony's tail, and I would have to wait 40 days before I could fix him. The Bishop says that during Lent we must abstain. That means getting even with people, as well as eating candy. One Easter Sunday the Lord is alive again and abstaining is over. That sure was good news to me. I sure sang Hallelujah as loud as I could this Easter. The big people drown us out, but I bet they heard me on the back seat this time. I waited for Neville to get out of church. For forty days he had been sticking his nose in my face and saying "Fraidy cat" to me. I folded up my new coat from Best & Co and put it down real nice on the church steps, and I put some pebbles in my mitten, and when Neville came out I said to him that I was going to lick them, and I said "One two three" that was to give him plenty of time. And I socked him just once good. And he ran screaming home, and his father brought him to our house to show his jaw to my mother. I mean Neville's jaw not his father's.

And I thought my mother would make me read my Bible until I was black in the face. But instead she beat me. My mother pounded on me until her pompadour bounced loose and her rat fell out. But I didn't care. I sure finished my unfinished business. Lent is over. The Lord is risen. Glory! Hallelujah! (The bishop's comment – most worthy abstinence.)

Local persons, in order of appearance

Betty Hangar and her daddy
Elizabeth Hanger, the only daughter of Harry and Elizabeth Hanger, was born on April 14, 1905. They lived in Richmond, KY. Mr. Harry Baylor Hanger was a well-known engineer, whose company Mason-Hanger built the Lincoln Tunnel and other major projects (*OYJ&J*, Betty Talbot)

Virginia's father
Richard Nathaniel Hudson, civil engineer. Residence on unnamed street in 1910 census, Versailles, Magisterial District 4, Witherspoon Precinct, Sheet 17A, #265/ 272. Biography in *Virginia Cary Hudson*

Milton H. Smith
President of L& N Railroad (1891-1921) (*OYJ&J*, Wilton Smoot) http://kdl.kyvl.org/catalog/xt731z41rt2k/text

(Edith) Hunter
born 1895, living on Rose Hill, Versailles, (no house number) in 1910 census. (*OYJ&J*, Mrs. Harris)

Pearl (Haggin) Margaret Pearl Voorhies,
living on Rose Hill, Versailles, (no house number) and in New York, NY; second wife of James Ben Ali Haggin; founder of Margaret Hall School. (*OYJ&J*, Ruby Porter) Biography in *Virginia Cary Hudson.*

John Morris
Possibly the John Morris born 1840, living on Nicholasville Pike, Childers, Ky. (no house number) in 1910 Census.

Neville Graddy
born 1896, living on Elm Street, Versailles, (no house number) in 1910 census. (*OYJ&J*, Nelson Brady)

Mrs. Powhatan Woolridge
Margaret Woolridge, born 1879, wife of Powhatan, living on Floydsburg Valley (no house no.), Beard Pct., Oldham County Ky. in 1910 census (*OYJ&J*, Mrs. Columbia Stonington)

Mr. Browning
Probably Charles M. Browning, born 1858, living on Elm St. (no house no.) in 1910 census (*OYJ&J*, Mr. Anderson, Mr. Hamilton)

Virginia's mother
Jessie Lee Gregory Hudson
Biography in *Virginia Cary Hudson.*

Family maid, Emma
Mother of Sallie

Mr. Moseley
There are many Moseleys in the 1910 Woodford Co. census. (*OYJ&J*, Mr. Sargent)

Mr. Mapother
Probably Wible L. Mapother, who served as president of the L & N Railroad (1921—1926) after Milton H. Smith's death

Harvey Steadman
born 1898, living on Montgomery Ave, Versailles in the 1910 Woodford Co.census
Dr. Sam Steadman, born 1869, living on Montgomery Ave, Versailles, Ky., in the 1910 census. Wife, Mary; sons: Worley (possibly an incorrect transcription of Harvey), born 1897, and Leander, born 1901. Dr. Steadman signed the death certificate of Infant Kirtley Cleveland, d. August 8, 1915. (*OYJ&J*, Dr. Reddings)

The Bishop (Burton)
Lewis W. Burton, Bishop of the Diocese of Lexington (1826-1929). See Frances Keller Barr, *Ripe to the Harvest: History of the Episcopal Diocese of Lexington 1895-1995*, Lexington, KY, 1995. (*OYJ&J*, Bishop Jordan)

Names used in *O Ye Jigs & Juleps!* are indicated with (*OYJ&J*).

I am grateful to Kathryn Bratcher, Associate Curator of Collections, Filson Historical Society, for identifying the residents of Versailles who appear in this essay.

More biographical information on Virginia's family members is found in Beverly Mayne Kienzle, *Virginia Cary Hudson, The Jigs & Juleps! Girl: Her Life and Writings.*

Additional photos and information about Virginia are found on jigsandjuleps.wordpress.com.

The author

Virginia Cary Hudson (May 28, 1894-April 8, 1954), a *New York Times* bestselling author from Kentucky, wrote a series of charming essays on southern life and religion as a 10-year-old in Versailles. Virginia's daughter, Virginia Cleveland Mayne, published the delightful essays as *O Ye Jigs and Juleps!* in 1962. The book reached the *New York Times Book Review*'s Best Seller List for 66 weeks and sold over a million copies. The title of the book is inspired by a traditional canticle, sung in Episcopal worship: "O ye children of men, Bless ye the Lord, Praise Him and Magnify Him Forever." Virginia's daughter published three more books of her mother's writings: *Credos & Quips* (1964); *Flapdoodle, Trust & Obey* (1966), a collection of Virginia's letters; and *Close Your Eyes When Praying* (1968), lessons about the Bible and the people in it, from a woman's point of view.

The editor

Beverly Mayne Kienzle, Ph.D., a retired Harvard Divinity School professor, has published numerous scholarly articles and books, including five on the medieval visionary, Hildegard of Bingen. Beverly is a granddaughter of Virginia Cary Hudson Cleveland (1894-1954), the author of *O Ye Jigs & Juleps!* Dr. Kienzle grew up surrounded by manuscripts as her mother tirelessly completed the publication of four volumes of Virginia Cary Hudson's writings. In 2016, Beverly published a delightful authoritative biography of her grandmother: *Virginia Cary Hudson, The Jigs & Juleps! Girl: Her Life & Writings*. After *Unfinished Business*, Beverly will publish other selected works by her grandmother. Virginia's lively spirit pervades all her writings, as she reveals her acute and humorous observations of humankind.